Richard Stevens,   United States Of America

The Declaration of Independence and Constitution of the United States of America

Richard Stevens,   United States Of America

The Declaration of Independence and Constitution of the United States of America

ISBN/EAN: 9783744660853

Printed in Europe, USA, Canada, Australia, Japan

Cover: Foto ©ninafisch / pixelio.de

More available books at **www.hansebooks.com**

THE

DECLARATION

OF

INDEPENDENCE

AND

CONSTITUTION

OF THE

UNITED STATES OF AMERICA.

NEW-YORK:

R. SPALDING.

1864.

DECLARATION

OF

INDEPENDENCE.

1776.

———

WHEN, in the courfe of human events, it becomes neceffary for one people to diffolve the political bands which have connected them with another, and to affume, among the powers of the earth, the feparate and equal ftation, to which the laws of nature, and of nature's God entitle them, a decent respect to the opinions of mankind requires that they should declare the causes which impel them to the separation.

We hold these truths to be self-evident --- that all men are created equal; that they are endowed by their Creator with certain inalienable rights; that among these are life, liberty, and the pursuit of happiness. That, to secure these rights, governments are instituted among men, deriving their just powers from the consent of the governed; that, whenever any form of government becomes destructive of these ends, it is the right of the people to alter or abolish it, and to institute a new government, laying its foundations on such principles, and organizing its powers in such form, as to them shall seem most likely to effect their safety and happiness.* Prudence, indeed, will dictate that governments long established should not be changed for light and transient causes; and, accordingly, all experience hath shown that mankind are more disposed to suffer, while evils are sufferable, than to right

themfelves by abolifhing the
forms to which they are accus-
tomed. But when a long train
of abufes and ufurpations, pur-
fuing invariably the fame object, evinces a defign to reduce
them under abfolute defpotifm,
it is their right, it is their duty,
to throw off fuch government,
and to provide new guards for
their future fecurity. Such
has been the patient fufferance
of thefe colonies, and fuch is
now the neceffity which con-
ftrains them to alter their for-
mer fyftems of government.
The hiftory of the prefent king
of Great Britain, is a hiftory

of repeated injuries and ufurpations, all having in direct
object the eftablifhment of an
abfolute tyranny over thefe
States. To prove this, let
facts be fubmitted to a candid
world.

He has refufed his affent to
laws the moft wholefome and
neceffary for the public good.

He has forbidden his gov-
ernors to pafs laws of immedi-
ate and preffing importance,
unlefs fufpended in their ope-
rations till his affent fhould be
obtained; and, when fo fus-
pended, he has utterly neg-
lected to attend to them.

He has refufed to pafs other laws for the accommodation of large diftricts of people, unlefs thofe people would re- linquifh the right of reprefen- tation in the Legiflature --- a right ineftimable to them, and formidable to tyrants only.

He has called together legis- lative bodies at places unufual, uncomfortable, and diftant from the repofitory of their public records, for the fole purpofe of fatiguing them into compli- ance with his meafures.

He has diffolved reprefen- tative houfes repeatedly, for oppofing, with manly firmnefs,

his invasions on the rights of
the people.

He has refused, for a long
time after such dissolutions, to
cause others to be elected,
whereby the legislative powers,
incapable of annihilation, have
returned to the people at large
for their exercise; the State
remaining, in the meantime,
exposed to all the dangers of
invasions from without, and
convulsions within.

He has endeavored to pre-
vent the population of these
States; for that purpose ob-
structing the laws for the naturalization of foreigners; refus-

ing to pafs others to encourage their migration hither, and raifing the conditions of new appropriations of lands.

He has obftructed the administration of juftice, by refufing his affent to laws for eftablifhing judiciary powers.

He has made judges dependent on his will alone for the tenure of their offices, and the amount and payment of their falaries.

He has erected a multitude of new offices, and fent hither fwarms of officers to harafs our people and eat out their subftance.

He has kept among us in times of peace, ſtanding armies, without the conſent of our Legiſlatures.

He has affected to render the military independent of, and ſuperior to, the civil power.

He has combined with others to ſubject us to a jurisdiction foreign to our conſtitutions, and unacknowledged by our laws; giving his aſſent to their acts of pretended legislation:

For quartering large bodies of armed troops among us;

For protecting them, by a mock trial, from puniſhment

for any murders which they
fhould commit on the inhabitants of thefe States;

* For cutting off our trade
with all parts of the world;

For impofing taxes on us
without our confent;

For depriving us, in many
cafes, of the benefit of trial by
jury;

For tranfporting us beyond
feas, to be tried for pretended
offences;

For abolifhing the free fys-
tem of Englifh laws in a neigh-
boring province, eftablifhing
therein an arbitrary government, and enlarging its boun-

daries, fo as to render it at once an example and fit inftrument for introducing the fame abfolute rule into thefe colonies;

For taking away our charters, abolifhing our moft valuable laws, and altering, fundamentally, the forms of our governments;

For fufpending our own Legiflatures, and declaring themfelves invefted with power to legiflate for us in all cafes whatfoever.

He has abdicated government here, by declaring us out

of his protection, and waging war againſt us.

He has plundered our ſeas, ravaged our coaſts, burned our towns, and deſtroyed the lives of our people.

He is at this time tranſporting large armies of foreign mercenaries, to complete the works of death, deſolation, and tyranny, already begun with circumſtances of cruelty and perfidy ſcarcely paralleled in the moſt barbarous ages, and totally unworthy the head of a civilized nation.

He has conſtrained our fellow-citizens, taken captive on

the high feas, to bear arms
againft their country, to become the executioners of their
friends and brethren, or to fall
themfelves by their hands.

He has excited domeftic in-
furrection among us, and has
endeavored to bring on the
inhabitants of our frontiers,
the mercilefs Indian favages,
whofe known rule of warfare
is an undiftinguifhed deftruc-
tion of all ages, fexes, and
conditions.

In every ftage of thefe op-
preffions we have petitioned for
redrefs in the moft humble
terms; our repeated petitions

have been anfwered only by
repeated injury. A prince
whofe character is thus marked
by every act which may define a tyrant, is unfit to be the
ruler of a free people.

Nor have we been wanting
in our attentions to our Britifh
brethren. We have warned
them, from time to time, of
attempts by their legiflature
to extend an unwarrantable
jurifdiction over us. We have
reminded them of the circum-
ftances of our emigration and
fettlement here. We have
appealed to their native juftice
and magnanimity, and we have

conjured them by the ties of
our common kindred, to dis-
avow thefe ufurpations, which
would inevitably interrupt our
connections and correfpon-
dence. They, too, have been
deaf to the voice of juftice
and of confanguinity. We
muft, therefore, acquiefce in
the neceflity which denounces
our feparation, and hold them
as we hold the reft of mankind
--- enemies in war --- in peace,
friends.

We, therefore, the repre-
fentatives of the United States
of America, in general Congrefs affembled, appealing to

the Supreme Judge of the world for the rectitude of our intentions, do, in the name and by the authority of the good people of thefe colónies, folemnly publifh and declare that thefe united colonies are, and of right ought to be, free and independent States; that they are abfolved, from all allegiance to the Britifh crown, and that all political connection between them and the ftate of Great Britain, is, and ought to be, totally diffolved, and that, as free and independent States, they have full power to levy war, conclude peace, contract alliances, eftablifh commerce, and do all other acts and things which independent States may of right do. And for the fupport of this Declaration, with a firm reliance on the protection of Divine Providence, we mutually pledge to each other our lives, our fortunes, and our facred honor.

The following is a list of the members of the Continental Congress, who signed the Declaration of Independence, with the places and dates of their birth, and the time of their respective deaths.

NAMES OF THE SIGNERS.	BORN AT		DELEGATE FROM	DIED.
Adams, John	Braintree, Mass.,	19th Oct., 1735.	Massachusetts,	4th July, 1826.
Adams, Samuel	Boston,	22d Sept., 1722.	Massachusetts,	2d Oct., 1803.
Bartlett, Josiah	Amesbury, "	in Nov., 1729.	New Hampshire,	19th May, 1795.
Braxton, Carter	Newington, Virginia,	10th Sept., 1736.	Virginia,	10th Oct., 1797.
Carroll, Charles of Carrollton	Annapolis, Md.,	20th Sept., 1737.	Maryland,	14th Nov., 1832.
Chase, Samuel	Somerset co., Md.,	17th April, 1741.	Maryland,	19th June, 1811.
Clark, Abraham	Elizabethtown, N. J.,	15th Feb., 1726.	New Jersey,	June, 1794.
Clymer, George	Philadelphia, Penn.,	in 1739.	Pennsylvania,	24th Jan., 1813.
Ellery, William	Newport, R. I.,	22d Dec., 1727.	Rhode Island and Prov. Plant.,	14th Feb., 1820.
Floyd, William	Suffolk co., N. Y.,	17th Dec., 1734.	New York,	4th Aug., 1821.
Franklin, Benjamin	Boston, Mass.,	17th Jan., 1706.	Pennsylvania,	17th April, 1790.
Gerry, Elbridge	Marblehead, Mass.,	17th July, 1744.	Massachusetts,	23d Nov., 1814.
Gwinnet, Button	England,	in 1732.	Georgia,	27th May, 1777.
Hall, Lyman	Connecticut,	in 1731.	Georgia,	Feb., 1790.
Hancock, John	Braintree, Mass.,	in 1737.	Massachusetts,	8th Oct., 1793.
Harrison, Benjamin	Berkely, Virginia,		Virginia,	April, 1791.
Hart, John	Hopewell, N. J.,	about 1715.	New Jersey,	1780.
Heyward, Thomas, Jr.	St. Luke's, S. C.,	in 1746.	South Carolina,	March, 1809.
Hewes, Joseph	Kingston, N. J.,	in 1730.	North Carolina,	10th Nov., 1779.
Hooper, William	Boston, Mass.,	in 1742.	North Carolina,	Oct., 1790.
Hopkins, Stephen	Scituate,	17th June, 1742.	Rhode Island and Prov. Plant.,	19th July, 1785.
Hopkinson, Francis	Philadelphia, Penn.,	7th March, 1747.	New Jersey,	9th May, 1790.
Huntington, Samuel	Windham, Conn.,	in 1731.	Connecticut,	5th Jan., 1796.
Jefferson, Thomas	Shadwell, Virginia,	2d July, 1722.	Virginia,	4th July, 1826.
Lee, Francis Lightfoot	Stratford,	13th April, 1745.	Virginia,	April, 1797.
Lee, Richard Henry	Stratford, "	14th Oct., 1734.	Virginia,	19th June, 1794.
Lewis, Francis	Landaff, Wales,	20th Jan., 1732.	New York,	30th Dec., 1803.
Livingston, Philip	Albany, N. Y.,	in March, 1713.	New York,	12th June, 1778.
Lynch, Thomas, Jr.	St. George's, S. C.,	15th Jan., 1716.	South Carolina,	lost at sea, 1779.
M'Kean, Thomas	Chester co., Penn.,	5th Aug., 1710.	Delaware,	24th June, 1817.

	Born		Died	
Middleton, Arthur	Middleton Place, S.C.	in 1743	1st Jan.,	1787
Morris, Lewis	Morrisania, N.Y.	in 1726	22d Jan.,	1798
Morris, Robert	Lancashire, England	Jan., 1733	8th May,	1806
Morton, John	Ridley, Penn.	in 1724	April,	1777
Nelson, Thomas, Jr.	York, Virginia	26th Dec. 1738	4th Jan.,	1789
Paca, William	Wye-Hill, Md.	31st Oct. 1740		1799
Paine, Robert Treat	Boston, Mass.	11th May, 1731	11th May,	1814
Penn, John	Caroline co., Virginia	in 1741	Sept.,	1788
Read, George	Cecil co., Md.	in 1734		1798
Rodney, Cæsar	Dover, Delaware	in 1728		1783
Ross, George	New Castle, Delaware	in 1730	July,	1779
Rush, Benjamin, M.D.	Byberry, Penn.	24th Dec. 1745	18th April,	1813
Rutledge, Edward	Charleston, S.C.	19th Nov. 1749	3d Jan.,	1800
Sherman, Roger	Newton, Mass.	in 1721	2d July,	1793
Smith, James	Ireland	in 1720	11th July,	1806
Stockton, Richard	Princeton, N.J.	1st Oct., 1730	26th Feb.,	1781
Taylor, George	Ireland	in 1716	5th Oct.,	1777
Thornton, Matthew	Ireland	in 1714	2d Feb.,	1803
Walton, George	Frederick co., Virginia	in 1740	2d Feb.,	1804
Whipple, William	Kittery, Maine	in 1730	28th June,	1785
Williams, William	Lebanon, Conn.	8th April, 1731	2d Aug.,	1811
Wilson, James	Scotland	about 1742	28th Aug.,	1798
Witherspoon, John	Yester, Scotland	5th Feb. 1722	15th Nov.,	1794
Wolcott, Oliver	Windsor, Conn.	26th Nov. 1726	1st Dec.,	1798
Wythe, George	Elizabeth City co., Va.	in 1726	8th June,	1806

Among the signers of the Declaration of Independence, were men engaged in almost every vocation. There were twenty-four LAWYERS; fourteen FARMERS, or men devoted chiefly to agriculture; nine MERCHANTS; four PHYSICIANS; one gospel MINISTER, and three who were educated for that profession, but chose other avocations; and one MANUFACTURER. A large portion of them lived to the age of three score and ten years. Three of them were over 90 years of age when they died; ten over 80; eleven over 70; fourteen over 60; eleven over 50; and six over 44. Mr. Lynch (lost at sea) was only 30.

John Hancock

Step Hopkins   Sam'l Adams

John Penn

Geo Read   Joseph Hewes

Th' Nelson jr   Geo Clymer

George Wythe

Fras Hopkinson

Benj' Harrison

Benjamin Rush

Rich'd Stockton

W'm Floyd   Edward Rutledge

Lewis Morris

Fran' Lewis   W'm Williams

Carter Braxton — Rob Morris

John Hart   James Wilson

Lyman Hall   John Morton

Tho Stone   Phil. Livingston

Richard Henry Lee

Geo Ross   Geo Walton.

Ja Smith   Wm Paca

Elbridge Gerry Benj. Franklin

Wm Whipple

Oliver Wolcott Caesar Rodney

          Thomas Lynch Junr

Geo Taylor

          Arthur Middleton

Wm Hooper

Francis Lightfoot Lee John Adams

Rob Treat Paine

Charles Carroll of Carrollton

Sam" Huntington

Tho' Heyward Jun

Abra Clark   Jno Witherspoon

Th Jefferson

Button Gwinnett

William Ellery

Matthew Thornton

Samuel Chase

Roger Sherman

Tho M: Kean   Josiah Bartlett

CONSTITUTION

OF THE

UNITED STATES.

WE the People of the United States, in order to form a more perfect union, eftablifh juftice, infure domestic tranquillity, provide for the common defence, promote the general welfare, and fecure the bleflings of liberty to ourfelves and our pofterity, do ordain and eftablifh this CONSTITUTION for the United States of America.

ARTICLE I.

SECTION 1. All legiflative powers herein granted fhall be vefted in a Congrefs of the United States, which fhall confift of a fenate and houfe of reprefentatives.

SECTION 2. The houfe of reprefentatives fhall be compofed of members chofen every fecond year by the people of the feveral States, and the electors in each State fhall have the qualifications requifite for electors of the moft numerous branch of the ftate legiflature.

No perfon fhall be a reprefentative who fhall not have

attained to the age of twenty-
five years, and been feven years
a citizen of the United States,
and who fhall not, when elected,
be an inhabitant of that ftate,
in which he fhall be chofen.

Reprefentatives and direct
taxes fhall be apportioned
among the feveral ftates which
may be included within this
Union, according to their respective numbers, which fhall
be determined by adding to
the whole number of free perfons, including thofe bound to
fervice for a term of years,
and excluding Indians not tax-
ed, three-fifths of all other

perfons. The actual enumeration fhall be made within
three years after the firft meeting of the Congrefs of the
United States, and within every
fubfequent term of ten years,
in fuch manner as they fhall
by law direct. The number
of reprefentatives fhall not exceed one for every thirty thoufand, but each State fhall have
at leaft one reprefentative; and
until fuch enumeration fhall be
made, the State of New Hamp-
fhire fhall be entitled to choofe
three, Maffachufetts eight,
Rhode Ifland and Providence
Plantations one, Connecticut

five, New York fix, New Jerfey four, Pennfylvania eight, Delaware one, Maryland fix, Virginia ten, North Carolina five, South Carolina five, and Georgia three.

When vacancies happen in the reprefentation from any ftate, the executive authority thereof fhall iffue writs of election to fill fuch vacancies.

The Houfe of Reprefentatives fhall choofe their fpeaker and other officers; and fhall have the fole power of impeachment.

SECTION 3. The Senate of the United States fhall be com-

pofed of two fenators from
each ftate, chofen by the legis-
lature thereof, for fix years;
and each fenator fhall have one
vote.

Immediately after they fhall
be affembled in confequence of
the firft election, they fhall be
divided as equally as may be
into three claffes. The feats
of the fenators of the firft
clafs fhall be vacated at the
expiration of the fecond year,
of the fecond clafs at the expiration of the fourth year,
and of the third clafs at the
expiration of the fixth year,
fo that one-third may be cho-

fen every fecond year; and if vacancies happen by refignation, or otherwife, during the recefs of the legiflature of any ftate, the executive thereof may make temporary appointments until the next meeting of the legiflature, which fhall then fill fuch vacancies.

No perfon fhall be a fenator who fhall not have attained to the age of thirty years, and been nine years a citizen of the United States, and who fhall not, when elected, be an inhabitant of that ftate for which he fhall be chofen.

The vice-prefident of the

United States ſhall be preſident of the Senate, but ſhall have no vote, unleſs they be equally divided.

The Senate ſhall chooſe their other officers, and alſo a preſident pro tempore, in the abſence of the vice-preſident, or when he ſhall exerciſe the office of preſident of the United States.

The Senate ſhall have the ſole power to try all impeachments: When ſitting for that purpoſe, they ſhall be on oath or affirmation. When the preſident of the United States is tried, the chief-juſtice ſhall preſide : and no perſon ſhall be convicted without the concurrence of two-thirds of the members preſent.

Judgment in caſes of impeachment ſhall not extend further than to removal from office, and diſqualification to hold and enjoy any office of honor, truſt or profit under the United States : but the party convicted ſhall neverthelefs be liable and ſubject to indictment, trial, judgment and puniſhment according to law.

SECTION 4. The times, places and manner of holding elections for ſenators and reprefentatives, fhall be prefcribed in each ftate by the legiflature thereof; but the Congrefs may at any time, by law, make or alter fuch regulations, except as to the places of choofing fenators.

The Congrefs fhall affemble at leaft once in every year, and fuch meeting fhall be on the firft Monday in December, unlefs they fhall by law appoint a different day.

SECTION 5. Each houfe fhall be the judge of the elections, returns and qualifications of its own members, and a majority of each fhall conftitute a quorum to do bufinefs; but a fmaller number may adjourn from day to day, and may be authorized to compel the attendance of abfent members, in fuch manner, and under fuch penalties as each houfe may provide.

Each houfe may determine the rules of its proceedings, punifh its members for difor-, derly behavior, and, with the concurrence of two-thirds, expel a member.

Each houfe fhall keep a journal of its proceedings, and from time to time publifh the fame, excepting fuch parts as may in their judgment require fecrecy, and the yeas and nays of the members of either houfe on any queftion fhall, at the defire of one-fifth of thofe prefent, be entered on the journal.

Neither houfe, during the feffion of Congrefs, fhall, without the confent of the other, adjourn for more than three days, nor to any other place than that in which the two houfes fhall be fitting.

SECTION 6. The fenators and reprefentatives fhall receive a compenfation for their fervices, to be afcertained by law, and paid out of the treafury of the United States. They fhall in all cafes, except treafon, felony and breach of the peace, be privileged from arreft during their attendance at the feffion of their refpective houfes, and in going to and returning from the fame; and for any fpeech or debate in either houfe, they fhall not be queftioned in any other place.

No fenator or reprefentative fhall, during the time for which he was elected, be appointed to any civil office under the authority of the United States, which fhall have been created, or the emoluments

whereof fhall have been increafed during fuch time;
and no perfon holding any
office under the United States,
fhall be a member of either
houfe during his continuance
in office.

SECTION 7. All bills for
raifing revenue fhall originate
in the Houfe of Reprefentatives; but the Senate may pro-
pofe or concur with amendments as on other bills.

Every bill which fhall have
paffed the Houfe of Reprefentatives and the Senate, fhall,
before it become a law, be
prefented to the prefident of

the United States; if he ap-
prove he fhall fign it, but
if not he fhall return it, with
his objections to that houfe in
which it fhall have originated,
who fhall enter the objections
at large on their journal, and
proceed to reconfider it. If
after fuch reconfideration, two-
thirds of that houfe fhall agree
to pafs the bill, it fhall be fent,
together with the objections to
the other houfe, by which it
fhall likewife be reconfidered,
and if approved by two-thirds
of that houfe, it fhall become
a law. But in all fuch cafes
the votes of both houfes fhall

be determined by yeas and nays, and the names of the perſons voting for and againſt the bill ſhall be entered on the journal of each houſe reſpectively. If any bill ſhall not be returned by the preſident within ten days (Sunday excepted) after it ſhall have been preſented to him, the ſame ſhall be a law, in like manner as if he had ſigned it, unleſs the Congreſs by their adjournment prevent its return, in which caſe it ſhall not be a law.

Every order, reſolution, or vote to which the concurrence of the Senate and Houſe of

Reprefentatives may be neces-
fary (except on a queftion of
adjournment) fhall be prefented
to the prefident of the United
States; and before the fame
fhall take effect, fhall be approved by him, or being dis-
approved by him, fhall be
repaffed by two-thirds of the
Senate and Houfe of Reprefentatives, according to the
rules and limitations prefcribed
in the cafe of a bill.

SECTION 8. The Congrefs
fhall have power to lay and
collect taxes, duties, impofts
and excifes, to pay the debts
and provide for the common

defence and general welfare of
the United States; but all
duties, impofts and excifes fhall
be uniform throughout the
United States;

₂ To borrow money on the
credit of the United States;

₃ To regulate commerce with
foreign nations, and among the
feveral ftates, and with the
Indian tribes;

₄ To eftablifh an uniform rule
of naturalization, and uniform
laws on the fubject of bank-
ruptcies throughout the United States;

₅ To coin money, regulate the
value thereof, and of foreign

coin, and fix the ſtandard of weights and meaſures;

To provide for the puniſh-ment of counterfeiting the ſe-curities and current coin of the United States;

To eſtabliſh poſt-offices and poſt-roads;

To promote the progreſs of science and uſeful arts, by ſecuring for limited times, to authors and inventors the ex-cluſive right to their reſpective writings and diſcoveries;

To conſtitute tribunals infe-rior to the ſupreme court;

To define and puniſh pira-cies and felonies committed on

the high feas, and offences
againſt the law of nations;

To declare war, grant letters of marque and repriſal,
and make rules concerning
captures on land and water;

To raiſe and ſupport armies,
but no appropriation of money
to that uſe ſhall be for a longer
term than two years;

To provide and maintain a
navy;

To make rules for the government and regulation of the
land and naval forces;

To provide for calling forth
the militia to execute the laws

of the Union, fupprefs infur-
rections and repel invafions;

16 To provide for organizing,
arming, and difciplining, the
militia, and for governing fuch
part of them as may be em-
ployed in the fervice of the
United States, referving to the
ftates refpectively, the appointment of the officers, and the
authority of training the militia
according to the difcipline prefcribed by Congrefs;

17. To exercife exclufive legislation in all cafes whatfoever,
over fuch diftrict (not exceeding ten miles fquare) as may,
by ceffion of particular ftates,

and the acceptance of Congrefs, become the feat of government of the United States,
and to exercife like authority
over all places purchafed by
the confent of the legiflature
of the ftate in which the fame
fhall be, for the erection of
forts, magazines, arfenals,
dockyards, and other needful
buildings ;--- And

₁₈ To make all laws which
fhall be neceffary and proper
for carrying into execution
the foregoing powers, and
all other powers vefted by this
conftitution in the government
of the United States, or in

any department or officer thereof.

Section 9. The migration or importation of fuch perfons as any of the ftates now ex-ifting fhall think proper to admit, fhall not be prohibited by the Congrefs prior to the year one thoufand eight hun-dred and eight, but a tax or duty may be impofed on fuch importation, not exceeding ten dollars for each perfon.

The privilege of the writ of habeas corpus fhall not be fufpended, unlefs when in cafes of rebellion or invafion the public fafety may require it.

No bill of attainder or ex poſt faĉto law ſhall be paſſed.

No capitation, or other di-reĉt, tax ſhall be laid, unleſs in proportion to the cenſus or enumeration hereinbefore di-reĉted to be taken.

No tax or duty ſhall be laid on articles exported from any ſtate.

No preference ſhall be given by any regulation of com-merce or revenue to the ports of one ſtate over thoſe of an-other: nor ſhall veſſels bound to, or from, one ſtate, be obliged to enter, clear, or pay duties in another.

No money fhall be drawn from the treafury, but in confequence of appropriations made by law; and a regular ftatement and account of the receipts and expenditures of all public money fhall be publifhed from time to time.

No title of nobility fhall be granted by the United States: And no perfon holding any office of profit or truft under them, fhall, without the confent of the Congrefs, accept of any prefent, emolument, office, or title, of any kind whatever, from any king, prince, or foreign ftate.

SECTION 10. No ftate fhall
enter into any treaty, alliance,
or confederation; grant letters
of marque and reprifal; coin
money; emit bills of credit;
make anything but gold and
filver coin a tender in payment
of debts; pafs any bill of attainder, ex poft facto law, or
law impairing the obligation
of contracts, or grant any title
of nobility.

No ftate fhall, without the
confent of the Congrefs, lay
any impoft or duties on imports
or exports, except what may
be abfolutely neceffary for
executing its infpection laws;

and the net produce of all duties and imposts, laid by any state on imports or exports, shall be for the use of the treasury of the United States; and all such laws shall be subject to the revision and control of the Congress.

No state shall, without the consent of Congress, lay any duty of tonnage, keep troops, or ships-of-war in time of peace, enter into any agreement or compact with another state, or with a foreign power, or engage in war, unless actually invaded, or in such imminent danger as will not admit of delay.

ARTICLE II.

SECTION 1. The executive power fhall be vefted in a prefident of the United States of America. He fhall hold his office during the term of four years, and, together with the vice-prefident, chofen for the fame term, be elected, as follows:

Each ftate fhall appoint, in fuch manner as the legiflature thereof may direct, a number of electors, equal to the whole number of fenators and reprefentatives to which the State may be entitled in the Congrefs: but no fenator or reprefentative, or perſon holding an office of truſt or profit under the United States, ſhall be appointed an electtor.

[The electtors ſhall meet in their reſpective ſtates, and vote by ballot for two perſons, of whom one at leaſt ſhall not be an inhabitant of the ſame ſtate with themſelves. And they ſhall make a liſt of all the perſons voted for, and of the number of votes for each; which liſt they ſhall ſign and certify, and tranſmit ſealed to the feat of the government of the United States, directed to the preſident of the Senate.

The prefident of the Senate fhall, in the prefence of the Senate and Houfe of Reprefentatives, open all the certificates, and the votes fhall then be counted.   The perfon having the greateft number of votes fhall be the prefident, if fuch number be a majority of the whole number of electors appointed; and if there be more than one who have fuch majority and have an equal number of votes, then the Houfe of Reprefentatives fhall immediately choofe by ballot one of them for prefident; and if no perfon have a majority, then

from the five higheft on the
lift the faid houfe fhall in like
manner choofe the prefident.
But in choofing the prefident,
the votes fhall be taken by
ftates, the reprefentation from
each ftate having one vote; a
quorum for this purpofe fhall
confift of a member or members from two-thirds of the
ftates, and a majority of all
ftates fhall be neceffary to a
choice. In every cafe, after
the choice of the prefident, the
perfon having the greateft
number of votes of the electors fhall be the vice-prefident.
But if there fhould remain two

or more who have equal votes, the Senate ſhall chooſe from them by ballot the vice-preſi-dent.]

The Congreſs may determine the time of chooſing the electors, and the day on which they ſhall give their votes; which day ſhall be the ſame throughout the United States.

No perſon except a natural born citizen, or a citizen of the United States, at the time of the adoption of this Conſti-tution, ſhall be eligible to the office of preſident; neither ſhall any perſon be eligible to that office who ſhall not have

attained to the age of thirty-
five years, and been fourteen
years a refident within the
United States.

In cafe of the removal of
the prefident from office, or of
his death, refignation, or inability to difcharge the powers
and duties of the faid office,
the fame fhall devolve on the
vice-prefident, and the Congrefs may by law provide for
the cafe of removal, death,
refignation, or inability, both
of the prefident and vice-prefident, declaring what officer
fhall then act as prefident, and
fuch officer fhall act accord-

ingly, until the difability be removed, or a prefident fhall be elected.

The prefident fhall, at ftated times, receive for his fervices, a compenfation, which fhall neither be increafed nor diminifhed during the period for which he fhall have been elected, and he fhall not receive within that period any other emolument from the United States, or any of them.

Before he enter on the execution of his office, he fhall take the following oath or affirmation: --- "I do folemnly fwear (or affirm) that I will faithfully execute the office of prefident of the United States, and will to the beft of my ability, preferve, protect and defend the conftitution of the United States."

SECTION 2. „ The prefident fhall be commander-in-chief of the army and navy of the United States, and of the militia of the feveral ftates, when called into the actual fervice of the United States; he may require the opinion, in writing, of the principal officer in each of the executive departments, upon any fubject relating to the duties of their refpective

offices, and he fhall have power
to grant reprieves and pardons
for offences againft the United
States, except in cafes of impeachment.

2 He fhall have power, by and
with the advice and confent of
the Senate, to make treaties,
provided two-thirds of the fenators prefent concur; and he
fhall nominate, and by and
with the advice and confent of
the Senate, fhall appoint ambaffadors, other public minis-
ters and confuls, judges of the
fupreme court, and all other
officers of the United States;
whofe appointments are not

herein otherwife provided for, and which fhall be eftablifhed by law; but the Congrefs may by law veft the appointment of fuch inferior officers, as they think proper, in the prefident alone, in the courts of law, or in the heads of depart-ments.

3 The prefident fhall have power to fill up all vacancies that may happen during the recefs of the Senate, by grant-ing commiffions which fhall expire at the end of their next feffion.

SECTION 3. He fhall from time to time give to the Congrefs information of the ftate of the Union, and recommend to their confideration fuch meafures as he fhall judge neceffary and expedient; he may, on extraordinary occafions, convene both houfes, or either of them, and in cafe of difagreement between them, with refpect to the time of adjournment, he may adjourn them to fuch time as he fhall think proper; he fhall receive ambaffadors and other public minifters; he fhall take care that the laws be faithfully executed, and fhall commiffion all the officers of the United States.

SECTION 4. The prefident, vice-prefident and all civil officers of the United States, fhall be removed from office on impeachment for, and conviction of, treafon, bribery, or other high crimes and mifdemeanors.

ARTICLE III.

SECTION 1. The judicial power of the United States, fhall be vefted in one fupreme court, and in fuch inferior courts as the Congrefs may from time to time ordain and eftablifh. The judges, both of the fupreme and inferior courts, ſhall hold their offices during good behavior, and ſhall, at ſtated times, receive for their ſervices, a compenſation, which ſhall not be diminiſhed during their continuance in office.

SECTION 2. The judicial power ſhall extend to all caſes, in law and equity, ariſing under this Conſtitution, the laws of the United States, and treaties made, or which ſhall be made, under their authority; --- to all caſes affecting ambaſſadors, other public miniſters, and conſuls; --- to all caſes of admiralty and maritime juriſdiction;---to controverfies to which the United States fhall be a party;---to controverfies between two or more ftates;--- between a ftate and citizens of another ftate;---between citizens of different ftates;---between citizens of the fame ftate claiming lands under grants of different ftates, and between a ftate, or the citizens thereof, and foreign ftates, citizens or fubjects.

In all cafes affecting ambas-fadors, other public minifters and confuls, and thofe in which a ftate fhall be party, the fupreme court fhall have original jurifdiction. In all the other cafes before mentioned, the fupreme court fhall have appellate jurifdiction, both as to law and fact, with fuch exceptions, and under fuch regulations as the Congrefs fhall make.

The trial of all crimes, except in cafes of impeachment, fhall be by jury; and fuch trial fhall be held in the State where the faid crime fhall have been committed; but when not committed within any ftate, the trial fhall be at fuch place or places as the Congrefs may by law have directed.

SECTION 3. Treaſon againſt the United States, ſhall conſiſt only in levying war againſt them, or in adhering to their enemies, giving them aid and comfort.

No perſon ſhall be convicted of treaſon unleſs on the teſtimony of two witneſſes to the ſame overt act, or on confeſſion in open court.

The Congreſs ſhall have power to declare the puniſhment of treaſon, but no attainder of treaſon ſhall work corruption of blood, or forfeiture except during the life of the perſon attainted.

ARTICLE IV.

SECTION 1. Full faith and credit fhall be given in each ftate to the public acts, records, and judicial proceedings of every other ftate. And the Congrefs may by general laws prefcribe the manner in which fuch acts, records and proceedings fhall be proved, and the effect thereof.

SECTION 2. The citizens of each ftate fhall be entitled to all privileges and immunities of citizens in the feveral ftates.

A perfon charged in any ftate with treafon, felony, or other crime, who fhall flee from juftice, and be found in another ftate, fhall on demand of the executive authority of the ftate from which he fled, be delivered up, to be removed to the ftate having jurifdiction of the crime.

No perfon held to fervice or labor in one ftate, under the laws thereof, efcaping into another, fhall, in confequence of any law or regulation therein, be difcharged from fuch fervice or labor, but fhall be delivered up on claim of the party to whom fuch fervice or labor may be due.

SECTION 3. New ftates may

be admitted by the Congrefs into this Union; but no new ftate fhall be formed or erected within the jurifdiction of any other ftate; nor any ftate be formed by the junction of two or more ftates, or parts of ftates, without the confent of the Legiflatures of the ftates concerned as well as of the Congrefs.

The Congrefs fhall have power to difpofe of and make all needful rules and regulations refpecting the territory or other property belonging to the United States; and nothing in this Conftitution

ſhall be ſo conſtrued as to pre-
judice any claims of the United States, or of any particular
ſtate.

SECTION 4. The United
States ſhall guaranty to every
ſtate in this Union, a republican
form of government, and ſhall
protect each of them againſt
invaſion, and on application of
the legiſlature, or of the executive (when the legiſlature can-
not be convened) againſt do-
meſtic violence.

ARTICLE V.

The Congreſs, whenever
two-thirds of both houſes ſhall

deem it neceſſary, ſhall propoſe amendments to this Conſtitution, or, on the application of the legiſlatures of two-thirds of the ſeveral ſtates, ſhall call a convention for propoſing amendments, which, in either caſe, ſhall be valid to all intents and purpoſes, as part of this Conſtitution, when ratified by the legiſlatures of three-fourths of the ſeveral ſtates, or by conventions in three-fourths thereof, as the one or the other mode of ratification may be propoſed by the Congreſs; provided that no amendment which may be made prior to the year one thoufand eight hundred and eight, fhall in any manner affect the firft and fourth claufes in the ninth fection of the firft article; and that no ftate, without its confent, fhall be deprived of its equal fuffrage in the Senate.

ARTICLE VI.

All debts contracted and engagements entered into, before the adoption of this Conftitution, fhall be as valid againft the United States under this Conftitution, as under the confederation.

This Conftitution, and the

laws of the United States which
fhall be made in purfuance
thereof; and all treaties made,
or which fhall be made, under
the authority of the United
States, fhall be the fupreme
law of the land; and the judges
in every ftate fhall be bound
thereby, anything in the conftitution or laws of any State
to the contrary notwithftand-
ing.

The fenators and reprefentatives before mentioned, and
the members of the feveral
ftate legiflatures, and all executive and judicial officers, both
of the United States and of

the feveral ftates, fhall be
bound by oath or affirmation,
to fupport this Conftitution;
but no religious teft fhall ever
be required as a qualification
to any office or public truft
under the United States.

Article VII.

The ratification of the conventions of nine ftates, fhall
be fufficient for the eftablifhment of this Conftitution between the ftates fo ratifying
the fame.

Done in convention by the unani-
mous confent of the States prefent
the feventeenth day of September

in the year of our Lord one thoufand feven hundred and eighty-
feven and of the independence
of the United States of America
the twelfth.   In witnefs whereof
we have hereunto fubfcribed our
names.

G. Washington

Prefident, and deputy from Virginia

WILLIAM JACKSON,
    Secretary.

AMENDMENTS

To the Conſtitution of the United States, ratified according to the proviſions of the fifth article of the foregoing conſtitution.

ARTICLE I. Congreſs ſhall make no law reſpecting an eſtabliſhment of religion, or prohibiting the free exerciſe thereof; or abridging the freedom of ſpeech, or of the preſs; or the right of the people peaceably to aſſemble, and to petition the government for redreſs of grievances.

ARTICLE II. A well-regulated militia, being neceſſary

to the fecurity of a free ſtate, the right of the people to keep and bear arms, ſhall not be infringed.

ARTICLE III. No foldier ſhall, in time of peace be quartered in any houſe, without the confent of the owner, nor in time of war, but in a manner to be prefcribed by law.

ARTICLE IV. The right of the people to be fecure in their perſons, houſes, papers, and effects, againſt unreaſonable fearches and feizures, ſhall not be violated, and no warrants ſhall iſſue, but upon probable cauſe, fupported by oath or

affirmation, and particularly
defcribing the place to be
fearched, and the perfons or
things to be feized.

ARTICLE V. No perfon fhall
be held to anfwer for a capital,
or otherwife infamous crime,
unlefs on a prefentment or
indictment of a grand jury,
except in cafes arifing in the
land or naval forces, or in the
militia, when in actual fervice
in time of war and public
danger; nor fhall any perfon
be fubject for the fame offence
to be twice put in jeopardy
of life or limb; nor fhall be
compelled in any criminal cafe

to be a witnefs againft himfelf, nor to be deprived of life, liberty, or property, without due procefs of law; nor fhall private property be taken for public ufe, without juft compenfation.

ARTICLE VI. In all criminal profecutions, the accufed fhall enjoy the right to a fpeedy and public trial, by an impartial jury of the ftate and diftrict wherein the crime fhall have been committed, which diftrict fhall have been previoufly afcertained by law, and to be informed of the nature and caufe of the accufation; to be confronted with the witneſſes againſt him; to have compulſory proceſs for obtaining witneſſes in his favor, and to have the aſſiſtance of counſel for his defence.

ARTICLE VII. In ſuits at common law, where the value in controverſy ſhall exceed twenty dollars, the right of trial by jury ſhall be preſerved, and no fact tried by a jury ſhall be otherwiſe re-examined in any court of the United States, than according to the rules of common law.

ARTICLE VIII. Exceſſive bail ſhall not be required, nor

exceſſive fines impoſed, nor cruel and unuſual puniſhments inflicted.

ARTICLE IX. The enumeration in the Conſtitution, of certain rights, ſhall not be conſtrued to deny or diſparage others retained by the people.

ARTICLE X. The powers not delegated to the United States by the Conſtitution, nor prohibited by it to the States, are reſerved to the ſtates reſpectively, or to the people.

ARTICLE XI. The judicial power of the United States ſhall not be conſtrued to extend to any ſuit in law or equity, commenced or profecuted againſt one of the United ſtates by citizens of another ſtate, or by citizens or ſubjects of any foreign ſtate.

ARTICLE XII. The electors ſhall meet in their refpective ſtates, and vote by ballot for preſident and vice-preſident, one of whom, at leaſt, ſhall not be an inhabitant of the fame ſtate with themſelves; they ſhall name in their ballots the perſon voted for as preſident, and in diſtinct ballots the perſon voted for as vice-preſident, and they ſhall make diſtinct liſts of all perſons voted

for as prefident, and of all
perfons voted for as vice-prefident, and of the number of
votes for each, which lifts they
fhall fign and certify, and trans-
mit fealed to the feat of the
government of the United
States, directed to the prefident
of the Senate; --- the prefident
of the Senate fhall, in the
prefence of the Senate and
House of Reprefentatives, open
all the certificates, and the
votes fhall then be counted; ---
the perfon having the greateft
number of votes for prefident,
fhall be the prefident, if fuch
number be a majority of the

whole number of electors appointed; and if no person have such majority, then from the persons having the highest numbers not exceeding three on the list of those voted for as president, the House of Representatives shall choose immediately, by ballot, the president. But in choosing the president, the votes shall be taken by States, the representation from each state having one vote; a quorum for this purpose shall consist of a member or members from two-thirds of the states, and a majority of all the states shall

be neceſſary to a choice. And
if the Houſe of Repreſenta-
tives ſhall not chooſe a preſident
whenever the right of choice
ſhall devolve upon them, before the fourth day of March
next following, then the vice-
preſident ſhall act as preſident,
as in the caſe of the death or
other conſtitutional diſability
of the preſident. The perſon
having the greateſt number of
votes as vice-preſident, ſhall
be the vice-preſident, if ſuch
number be a majority of the
whole number of electors appointed, and if no perſon have
a majority, then from the two

higheſt numbers on the liſt, the Senate ſhall chooſe the vice-preſident; a quorum for the purpoſe ſhall conſiſt of two-thirds of the whole number of ſenators, and a majority of the whole number ſhall be neceſſary to a choice. But no perſon conſtitutionally ineligible to the office of preſident ſhall be eligible to that of vice-preſident of the United States.